Sending you joyful hugs this Easter.

May all of your dreams

and wishes come true.

smile eggs
Happy
Easter
sun
love
HAPPY
EGG
life
bunny
joy
good
chicken
spring

Aunt,

Wishing you an Easter that is bright,

happy, and full of contentment.

Hoppy Easter!

Sand-hill Cranes, Robins, and Red winged
blackbirds will sing,
Meeting together for the arrival of spring!

Hope your Easter is bright with color,
sweet with treats, and warm with sunshine!

Aunt,

May the hope of spring

bring days that are filled with joy,

laughter, and good times!

Wishing you an Easter that is as sweet

and special as you are!

Easter is more than just eggs and candy.

It is also about peace, love, and family.

Aunt,

I'm thinking of you and wishing you a

warm and wonderful bunny day!

Delivering hugs, kisses, and Easter
wishes just for you!

Thinking of you this season of renewal
& wishing you happiness at Easter &
throughout the year.

Here's hoping your spring is filled with
the beauty of nature.

Aunt,

May your Easter holiday bring you health, happiness, and lots of love!

Happy Easter

from Florabella Publishing, LLC